A
Stripper's Road
to
Recovery

SHEDDING THE LAYERS OF HEALING

Lisa Dunn

PRINT ISBN: 978-1-66783-167-1

CHAPTER 1

I was hungry. I was so tired of being hungry. I was so hungry.
I was too afraid to spend more than $2 on a cheeseburger and fries at my
job working at the movie theater. If I spent more than $2 on food then I was
worried I wouldn't have gas for my car, shampoo, and food for the next day.
I made my way back to the house, in Springfield Ohio. I was 17 staying with
the lady that let me live in the upstairs, who occasionally gave me Southern
Comfort alcohol to ease my pain. Another night making $5.15 an hour
wearing the same 2 popcorn smelling shirts, and trying to make whatever
money I had stretch for 2 weeks between food, toiletries, gas money and
insurance. Thank God this lady let me sleep at her house. I went to school
with her son and Junior high. She *was* a nice lady, but a control freak that
love taking in strays.

Yes, I'm calling myself a stray. I was a stray. I needed some place to
live and she was willing to let me stay there as long as I needed. I only live
with her for about a year from 16 to 17. That was a long time to live in one
place considering my background of living in poverty. I was safe and alone.
I could ask for more It was warm during the winter and she didn't ask me
a lot of questions. She just let me sleep in this room where her daughter
graduated high school and moved out of. It was September finally my senior
year of high school I was so excited to be done after changing high School
5 times in 3 years because of all the moving around as a kid. I was so close
to being finished. By then I had moved five times living with four different
families. Different beds, different rules it was all so confusing. I wasn't a bad
kid I just needed someone to put a roof over my head until I was 18. It was
September and in 2 weeks I was going to turn 18 years old. I was so excited

because then I could get a job that paid more and then I could get my own place and not have to rely on anybody. Relying on people didn't work very well for me. So I learned real early that I'd you don't rely on other people, you won't be disappointed. Hmmmm what job could I get?

I heard about a local telemarketing company that hired and paid $10 an hour if you were 18 years old. So I went to the telemarketing company that week and asked if they would hire me in 2 weeks so I could get a good paying job and get my own place. The lady told me the working hours are 8:00 a.m. to 4:00 p.m. Monday through Friday. I asked her if there was a second shift position because I was in high school; and I wanted to finish high school. She said unfortunately there's not a second shift position so I couldn't work there and be in high school at the same time, that wasn't an option.

Disappointed I went back to the movie theater for another 6-hour shift living on a $2 dinner meal to get me through the night. I started asking coworkers if they had any ideas. Some people talked about working at a restaurant but they said that's really hard work and people can be real mean. And then someone told me about exotic dancing. They said they knew someone that can make $500 a night on the weekend and they only work two days a week. Wow that was a lot of money to think about. And it would only be weekends so I could finish high School. It goes against everything I was taught though. My dad being a pastor when I was a kid wanted me to be moral and do the right thing. But after he was diagnosed schizophrenic when I was 10 and my mom diagnosed bipolar there was no one to help lead the way after that. My dad was gone I only saw him on a holiday or when he had time to meet me at the park. My mom slept all the time because that's the only way she knows how to cope with life. I don't blame her; I'd sleep too.

So early on I was taught the Bible Christian do the right thing, but now I'm just hungry. I'm tired. I want my own place to sleep. I want to make the rules. I'm tired of being told what to do by people that don't know what they're doing! Then they question what I'm doing and I'm just trying to survive. So everything I was taught didn't seem to help me. They didn't take care of me, didn't provide for me and it didn't keep me safe. Now I'm about to be 18 years old and I can do anything I want. But Being a stripper? A stripper? What the hell was I thinking how could I even consider doing something like that taking off my clothes for money, I 'm still a virgin! I'm never even had sex before.

But I'm so desperate. I'm so desperate to be taken care of myself! I know no one else will take care of me. I learned that 10 years ago. I learned that when Dad wasn't around whether he was working or after the divorce. Then Mom was in bed my entire life. It was up to me to take care of my little brother and sister. That's all I know, is how to take care of myself and other people that's what I've done my whole life. I learned in childhood that I have to take care of you, so that you will take care of me. I got to make you feel better so that I get my needs met.

After thinking about it doesn't sound like such a bad gig. Two nights a week I could take care of myself and finish high school. That sounds amazing really. Well I don't know where to go who would I talk to. So I asked my friend Brad the one that suggested it. He was a coworker at the movie theater and frankly the weed dealer of the county. I asked him where to go if I wanted to do something like that.

He offered to take me up to a place called Cheeks in Dayton, Ohio. He said he was willing to go with me just to help me out. Little did I know he really just wanted a chance to sit and look at all the women of course but I was naive and desperate.

So I thought about it for the next two weeks tossing and turning in bed at night. Periodically drinking some of the Southern comfort that I could find in the kitchen, that the lady would leave around for me. The more I thought about it though the more sense. I might be able to buy a whole meal and eat it at the same time. Instead of buying a meal and trying to figure out how to make it last one whole day.

I continued working in the movie theater behind the popcorn stand My shoes that are falling apart at the bottom souls coming off my little black Mary Jane shoes. My buttered popcorn smelling shirt and the maroon apron I always had on over top of trying to be presentable.

The weekend came at the movie theater, the police officers that secure the cinema asked me how I was doing. I said I was doing okay but I was trying to figure out what kind of job I could get at 18 so I can make enough money to take care of myself. I told him that someone told me about being as a stripper but I didn't know if that was a good idea. I hinted at asking him to share his opinion about whether it was a good idea or not.

"What do you think Travis, do you think I would be a good stripper?" I asked .

Travis, the cop, looked at me, looked me up and down and said "You would do just fine. You're pretty young girl, if they like you, you can make a lot of money doing it. I know a lot of girls that do that. And all those girls make a lot of money. The thing you got to be careful of is all that drinking. You don't want to drink and drive or do drugs because that'll get you in trouble with law enforcement. But if you can just go there and make your money and leave you're all set. I think you'd be real good at it! Just be careful you don't become a drunk; that's where you get in trouble.

Gosh another person that said that it could be a good idea and the more I spin that idea around the more interesting it sounded. My birthday fell on a Tuesday so I asked my friend Brad if he would take me to Cheeks on Friday after school.

He said "Heck yeah, I'll take you up there. I'll bring all my friends to support you too!"

I was scared, relieved, confused, excited lost, and anxious; but I'll do anything. I was so tired of being sick and tired. I just needed to make enough money to take care of myself, then I wouldn't have to worry about anything else in the world I would be okay.

The school week went by I fell asleep in first and second period of class as usual because I wasn't getting enough sleep at night. I survived another week tired and malnutritioned, but I got through it again. The only thing that comforted me was taking hot showers and hot baths. Heat, I learned real young was comforting and calmed me down when I was upset. When I hug the seat of a chair or the toilet I would feel safe and cared for. I just need something to lay my head and chest on to hold, and that made me feel better; I even felt happy sometimes. That's all I needed for comfort is a hot shower or a chair to hold and I felt better. Those hot showers were like someone hugging me, I felt calm, safe and relaxed. Getting a hot shower or a hot bath and all that warmth goes all over your body you can feel it migrate from the outside in! That's what a hug does only there is no one there to hug me or tell me it was going to be okay or hold me. But that's okay because no one ever did that before so I didn't realize I was missing anything at the time. But let me tell you that hot shower and hot bath, warmed me, comforted me and told me everything was going to be okay and that's all I needed. I just needed comfort and whenever I got comfort from heat,it increase my endorphins and when that happens I feel better! I feel okay. So even though I didn't get the kind of affection that most kids did I still got comforted it was just in a different way and that's how I survived. Best part about growing up on government assistance is the government pays for hot water. So as a child I got all the hot water I wanted. Growing up that's what made everything okay that's how I felt safe and comforted. When I was in a hot water.

The next weekend came and then myself and two of Brad's friends loaded up in the car and headed out, taking 70 West! I was so excited I had hope! Hope was something I hadn't had for a very very long time. Finally had hope for a better life!

CHAPTER 2

Brad, myself and 3 guyfriends drove west. We arrived at the club; it was so dark. When I walked in I saw a lady up front sitting by the cash register. Herr blonde hair to the side, olive skin wearing half a t-shirt with a slit down the front to show her bouncy boobs and a jean skirt. I couldn't see any lower than that because of the countertop. There were neon lights everywhere and one above her head said Cheeks! I told her I was interested in being a dancer but I didn't know how to do it. She asked to see my ID. I showed her my identification.

"I just turned 18 years old so I was ready to try something new." I said enthused but timid.

She looked me up and down and said, "Hang on let me call the manager."

About 5 minutes later a stocking man walked up. He looked like he was an ex- football player real broad shoulders and a belly. He was about 5'11 Ginger brown hair and a glossy glare with his brown eyes.

He leaned his elbow on the counter and positioned himself. Look me up and down said, "You want to be a dancer?"

I said "Yeah I want to be a dancer, but I don't know how to do it. I don't know what to do."

With his swag of confidence he turned his back and had me follow him. He took me through the busy long bar area that made a huge oval. I walked past so many men. It's crowded I felt like I was bumping into people just trying to walk through the aisle. There's beer everywhere neon lights everywhere; it was so dark. I couldn't get over how dark everything felt. But

6

I just kept following him and with him looking like a ex-football player he kind of moved people in the room. Whether he meant to or not. We got to the stage and I looked up.

"So this is what dancers do. They get on stage and dance. You walk up on that side of the stage when you get up there you take off your top. You don't take everything off on that side because you want to leave something for them to think about till you get to the other side. So on that side you take off your top, you do your dance for one song. You get your tips you can make full contact with the men just don't put your your crotch in their face and don't put your crotch on their crotch I don't want to see any of that. That's for the lap dance room. You understand? "

"Yes." I said not even knowing what's going on just looking up at these model women that are glowing in the dark, their tans all over their body. Yes, is the only thing I could think to say.

He proceeded, "Now when you get to the other side of the stage that's when you can take off your bottoms now you want to keep your thong on because this is a topless club. You don't want to take the whole thing off. If you got a top and a skirt, you take the top off on one side and the shorts or the skirt off on the other side of the stage. If you wear a dress you take the top part of the dress off on that side and then the whole dress off on the other side but you have to keep your thong on. So you get to the second part of the stage take everything off except for your thong, dance to the song you can collect your money's same rules apply to both sides. You're on stage for two songs. Do you think that's something you can do?"

With more confidence I replied, "Well yeah it looks easy enough, but what do I wear. Those clothes look so fancy. I don't know what to wear?"

"Well you could wear a nice pair of bra and underwear set."

"what does that look like l," I asked.

"Hang on let me go find you a magazine," He responded .

So he went and found one of the magazines. It has all the local adult store clothes and lingerie in it. He started flipping through and he said

"This kind of lingerie or that kind of outfit will work." The manager suggested.

I said "Oh so just like a really tight small dress would that work?"

"Yep, that would work. A lot of the girls wear bra and panty sets or bra and skirt set lingerie. Or if you have a nice tight short dress that would work too. Well, you go ahead and stay here and look through this magazine. If you want to give this a try, you come back and I'll put you on that stage and see if you can do it."

The music was so loud I felt lost in a crowd of men I was sitting at the bar looking at the magazine flipping through it. Well, I was desperate. I needed help. I needed a place to live. I wanted to eat a whole meal. All I could fantasize about is making sure the electric and gas stayed on and that I had hot water again. That's when I knew my answer I was ready to take care of myself and this is how I was going to do it.

I had my friends take me back home after they got 20 minutes of looking at the show and all the beautiful girls half naked.

That night, i looked through my clothes that I had at this lady's house. Everything I had fit in a plastic storage tub I lived out of for the last 3 years. I found one thing, it was a dark turquoise but part of the laces were kind of fraid you can tell it was clearly falling apart with the elastic starting to shred. It's the only thing that look semi attractive. I actually stole them from my older sister 4 years ago. All my other underwear were just full fruit of the loom panties. I needed a thong so I decided to use the dark lace ripped thong that I stole from my older sister so that I had something nice to wear at the strip club. Then, I started looking at my clothes none of my bras were good they were worn out, most of them are sports bras and I didn't have any booty shorts. Wait a minute, i found a prom dress I remember my junior prom. I wore a real long tight black prom dress. And the back was open with some fake diamond studs that had already fallen out. I know it's not perfect and I've had it for a while, but maybe I could cut it off to my butt. Yeah, that's what I'll do I'll cut off my prom dress from last year. That's what I'll do!

I got out the scissors I was so excited! I cut it off the best that I could and looked in the mirror. No that's not short enough. So I cut more off so that the bottom part of my butt cheeks were right at the bottom part of the dress. Yeah that's right now I look like a stripper! I called my friend and asked her if I could borrow 20 bucks because I needed a pair of black go-go boots. So the next day I went to a cheap thrift store and found some black go-go boots. I was so excited I was now completely ready to go audition to be a stripper! I'm on my way to freedom, there was hope for me yet!!

CHAPTER 3

THE AUDITION

I arrived back at cheeks that Friday night ready to audition I had my bag with my black boots, my black tight cut off prom dress with spaghetti straps and heart full of hope with nothing to lose.

When I got to the same cashier again walking in through the entrance everything was dark just like before only more men and more people were around. It was so loud is rap music pounding. My heart was racing but my head knew that I didn't have another any other choice. I was hungry, tired and alone.

The lady radioed on a walkie-talkie to the manager "There's a girl back to audition."

Just like previously 5 minutes went by and the manager showed up at the front where I was standing awkwardly toes pointed inward holding my bag for dear life not knowing what was going to happen next but having nothing to lose and only hope to gain.

"So you're ready to try this out?" He stated as if I had any other option.

"Yes I want to audition now. Just tell me what to do and I'll do it. "

Okay he said follow me. He sounded irritated one more person that he was going to run through the drill, but he was willing to give me a chance and I knew that if he gave me a chance I would do the best that I could, with what I got anyway.

I followed him to the girls dressing room where girls were staring at themselves in the mirror putting on makeup posing for themselves trying to feel pretty and get up the courage to go back out there. Some girls were walking around in their thongs others had their small tight fitted outfit on. Everyone was taller than I was I was 5 ft 0 weighing it 125 lb. So everything and everyone just seems like it was towering over me. My feelings of fear and anxiety were masked with hope and courage.

"Go ahead and change your clothes real quick. I dropped my bag quickly by the old gray locker with multiple scuff marks. I quickly took off my top and my bottoms. I put my cut prom dress on and black go-go boots. I brush my hair once. He showed me a locker to put my things in. There was no lock but at least my stuff wasn't out in the open. So I just left it in there and follow them out to the main room with the giant stage and two long silver poles. Okay remember the rules you get up on that side of the stage you take off your top or the top part of your dress for one song and dance and then you get to the other side of the stage for the next song and you take the whole thing off but you have to keep your song on got it? Yes what do you like to dance to? I like to dance to pop music or hip hop. What's your stage name? Stage name I didn't know I needed a stage name so I can't use my real name crap what do I do what name do I use. The only thing I could think of is when I was a little kid someone used to sing to me CC my playmates come down and play with me. Yeah I was the kids song CC my playmates CC my name will be cc! Coming up with it on the fly I said my name is CeCe. Okay pop music CC got it I'll go tell the dj. The song came on they announced my name CC. I felt so awkward I grabbed a hold of the bar next to me to walk up the stairs to the stage there's only four or five stairs but it felt like a tower especially when I got to the top I grabbed a hold of the pole I looked around in the all the darkness you could still see all the men staring at me. Some of them were lean back in their chair drinking a beer that they were tired from a long day of work, others were sitting on the edge of their seat wondering who I was and what I had to offer, and then there were the one sitting at the stage just waiting for someone to put their butt or boobs in their face so they can get in on the action for a dollar or two. Well here we go here it goes to Hope and freedom! I was so nervous my dance moves real quick short I didn't know what I was doing so I just wiggled my way around the pole sometimes trying to drop it like it's Hot considering that was only dance move I had from being in the bars. Then I got to the next side of the stage the dress came off still nervous still uncomfortable but excited and confused. I kept moving fast cuz that's all I knew how to do is shake it like it's Hot and drop it like it's Hot. That's all I knew how to do. The audition was over I could breathe finally came down from the three or four step staircase I was standing on the ground thankfully I had survived now I have to find out if I passed the test. Well what did you think he asked with a gruff voice wanting my approval that I would be willing to do it over and over again no matter what the cost. It was fun I was really nervous but it was fun being up there. But you know what I think he said as if I had a choice to answer. I think you need to slow down your moves a little bit if you slow down I got something that'll help you out. Rachel he hollered at the bartender give me a shout at 1:51 and a coke to Chase it. She quickly filled two plastic cups one with a healthy shot of 151 and the other with half a cup of Coke. He said here drink this but the key is you got to drink it real fast and one shot. Otherwise it's going to hurt and you might get sick. So just tilt your head back drink it in one goat and then drink some this coke right after it to chase it down. So I did is that exactly as he ordered I poured the 151 down my throat oh my gosh did that burn it was like I was burning from the inside out started with the back of my throat all the way down to my esophagus I chased that sucker down so fast without Coke so I didn't throw up. I stood there for a minute trying to brace myself my face Howard I touch my throat and my chest wondering what just happened to me and why I feel like my insides is burning from the inside out. On fire so to speak and then it happened. My whole body was hugged for the first time from the inside out. It was like one giant hug from the inside out it just held on I felt so loved. So wanted and so loved for the first time. Oxytocin was produced in my body when that alcohol hit oxytocin is the same hormone that's released when you feel loved wanted and affection. And now oxytocin has been released after that first shot of 151 and I felt loved and wanted for the first time in my entire life. And it came from a drink. Okay he said what do you think about that how do you feel? I said oh my God I feel amazing can I have another? He smiled gave me a big look of approval like and not at his head absolutely darling we'll get you another one and so I had one more. Wow I not only was going to about to make money but I felt loved and wanted for the first time in my life it was a beautiful thing. And that moment all the hope had been restored to my soul I was going to be okay and I was going to feel okay too. There's the beginning to the end.

6 months went by and not 6 month time frame I got my own apartment, put all the utilities in my name, fix my car that was broken down, bought me a whole new wardrobe, I had more food in the fridge that I knew what to do with, I was drinking feeling good all the time started smoking weed with my friends that like to hang out with me all the time. It was a beautiful thing I was finally self-sufficient finally had a place that someone couldn't take away from me I had slept in the same bed for 6 months continuously, I felt better and my needs were finally met. I had friends around me or so I thought. We all almost live together in this one little one bedroom apartment I was in. We just smoked weed all day watch TV at night and I would work on Friday and Saturday night. I decided to drop out of high school because high School wasn't doing me any good it was getting in the way of me enjoying my life. So that's what I did I dropped out of high school I'm just started living my life the way I wanted to. And taking care of myself the way I always dreamed of it was beautiful at least for that time.

Then one day I was in the back getting dressed for work my boss came to me said CeCe you can't drink anymore. The police are coming in undercover and if we have any underage drinkers in here they're going to give us big fine and I don't have time for that. So you can't drink anymore you have to stop if I catch you drinking you're fired. So I decided to start putting vodka and water bottles. Vodka is clear water is clear it only made sense to me. So that's what I did I started bringing in vodka so I can drink while I was at work. I thought as long as they didn't catch me drinking out there then they wouldn't know. But then one day it happened. They had a tanning bed inside the girls locker room. I laid down to tan and I passed out. It wasn't the first time it happened but this time I was woken up to my boss and CeCe get your ass out here right now! Are you drinking again I said no he said you're drunk you're drunk right now you need get dressed and get your ass out of here right now you've got me in enough trouble you owe me $400 for the last time that you drank you haven't given it to me yet. So you get your ass out of here right now I don't have time for underage drinkers around here! Well I couldn't really argue with that I was too drunk too anyway so I changed my clothes out got myself together and I left I sat in my car thinking to myself what the hell what do I do now I need a job. So I made my way home somehow safely thank the Lord. When I got home I started thinking well what do I do I need a job so I decided to look Brown at other clubs. I know if underage drinking is a problem I can find a fake ID and employ myself with a fake id. So that's what I did

I don't know what I was thinking because even though I was of age I still had a drunken attitude problem. After getting fired from four different clubs and Dayton Ohio because of my drunkenness my bad attitude and my violent threats to other girls, I decided that I'm running out of options and dayton. I at least knew one thing that dancing was for me it was taking care of all of my needs and so much more. But my drinking problem had already gotten out of control within the 6 months I had started. I decided to try sobering up I started running for 30 minutes a day, I quit hanging out with friends mainly because they kept stealing from me and I was tired of not knowing if I could trust people. It was easier just to keep everyone out. I had already had my apartment burglarized when I went out of town. I came back missing a CD player money stereo system. So I knew at that time moving forward I didn't want anyone in my house cuz I couldn't trust anyone, and I can only drink when I wasn't at work. Cuz anytime I drink I seem to get fired. Didn't matter whether I was had a fake ID and was of age or not I seem to be my big mouth kept getting me in trouble and I can't keep my mouth shut when I'm drunk.

I finally made my way to Columbus Ohio looking for a new area to work hoping that I didn't don't burn any new bridges. I found the club it was upscale and I had the audition and a certain time frame Monday through Friday between 4:00 and 7:00. Standards huh wasn't used to that. But okay so I made my audition got the job as usual and started working. Only this time the manager let me know very quickly within the first month if I drink on the job and if you catch me drunk or drinking he would have to fire me. He let me know that up front. For the first time I realized I've had to move to a whole new city just to function and I didn't want to screw this up. This is my only opportunity I found to take care of myself. So somehow I found a way to cooperate. When I noticed is all the underage girls there drink Red Bull so that's what I started doing as long as I had something to sip on so I felt like I was doing something then I was okay to not drink. Plus at this club there were more rules and the men weren't allowed to touch you I didn't feel the need to drink. Thing one day so I was at the club I met someone he was pharmaceutical sales rep he was young his in-law School and he was giving me lots of money. He invited me over to play pool with him at his house afterwards. Normally I say notice things like that but at this point I don't need too many sophisticated I had met too many sophisticated men in my life I decided to take the opportunity to be around someone sophisticated. I went to his house that night and I played pool with him we had a really good time and there was no pressure for any extra curricular activities it was just nice to enjoy somebody's company that seemed to have their life together. And I was in a new city Columbus seemed really nice especially on the North end where I stay where he stayed. So he invited me to move in with him and quit my dancing job. Holy cow what a great opportunity a sophisticated man wanting me to quit my dancing job live with him and he'll take care of me heck yeah man I went for it! I finally reached the next level I no longer had to take care of myself cuz I found someone who will take care of me!

I'm so excited about the idea that someone might actually care about me. Plus with all the oxytocin being produced in my brain from meeting someone and being in the honeymoon phase I thought sky was the limit. So I moved in with him and decided to go to real estate school. Who's the school close to where he lived and I can get my real estate school done in 3 weeks. So that's what I decided to do I was going to quit dancing and become a real estate agent. The weeks went by I went to real estate School quit my dancing job and started playing the wifey at home. I wasn't very good at it considering I drank all of his liquor all day long and in the evening I was coherent long enough to have sex with him when he got home from work before I passed out. One day I decided I'm going to put the past behind me I'm no longer an exotic dancer this is exciting I'm going to cut off all my hair! I'm going to start my new life with a new look. So that's what I did I went to Great clips have them give me a Halle Berry haircut which that's what everyone compared me to anyway it's Halle Berry because of my facial features now I have the short dark pixie cut to go with it. My olive skin color was glowing with rest and hope for another level level of life. One day I wanted to leave and go visit a girlfriend of mine. But he said I couldn't go. I thought to myself I don't need your permission to go visit a friend. He said if you live in my house under my roof you follow my rules you're not allowed to go anywhere unless I approve. I was so confused but he was taking care of me and we did live in a real fancy condo on the nicest part of columbus. Well maybe it's not that big of a deal I didn't see my friend in a while anyway so it wouldn't be that big of a deal if I didn't leave. So I just went upstairs and lay down for a little while cuz I didn't know what else to do I wasn't allowed to leave. When I went up there I started getting upset, what can he do to stop me. So I decided to get my purse get my things together and walk out the door. That made sense I'll prove a point he can and can't do! He was sitting on the couch I had to walk through the living room to get to the front door. He said where are you going said I want to go visit my friend said I said. He said I told you you can't go anywhere. The next thing you know he got up and he blocked the doorway I was halfway through the kitchen when he blocked the doorway from the other side. You're not leaving here and he had both of his hands on both sides of the door frame and instead in the way blocking the door. I grabbed the door handle I want to leave and then he moved so that my hand came off the door handle no you're not leaving! That was the garage exit which I usually go in and out of. But there's still the front door. So I darted towards the other door and he was so fast and so strong he got in front of the other door before I could even get to it. So now the front door is blocked. I told you you're not leaving you're not going anywhere! What you can't stop me. His voice got louder his shoulders arched up intimidating me. And he grabbed both door frames to clarify that I was not going anywhere! I felt so confused scared I froze. He's literally physically blocking the end of the house so I tried to push him out of the way by grabbing one side of his shoulder and his side to move him. He beefed up even higher even stronger even though he wasn't much bigger than I was I felt like such a child all of a sudden his anger Rose his voice deepened and louder and his physical appearance was terrifying as I realized he's not going to let me out of the house I couldn't get out there was no way. I thought maybe if I just run to the other door one more time so I ran back to the other door in the kitchen where the garage was. But as soon as I grab the handle and tried to open it up his hand bashed the door closed and he locked it and he stood blocking the doorway again you're not going anywhere I said! After the third attempt and 30 minutes of trying to get out and his anger and control towering over me I finally recoiled and decided he was right he was stronger than I was faster than I was and I finally realized I wasn't going anywhere. So just like a punished dog I tucked my tail between my legs put my head down submitted and walked back through the living room up the stairs into the bedroom and laid down I was so sad but as I sat there laying I realized well he is taking care of me we do live on a nice end of town he is a sophisticated man I probably wouldn't get much better than this anyway. So I tried to rationalize myself into thinking that my situation was so much better than I thought I just had to look at it that way. Now or later he came up stairs to the bedroom your wrap his arm laid down beside me in the bed and wrapped his arms around me and said I'm so sorry I got so angry with you I don't mean to I just care about you so much and I want to spend as much time with you as I can cuz I you're so important to me are you okay? I told him I was fine but I couldn't look at him I didn't want to snuggle or anything I just felt confused. I equated a sophisticated man to be someone that knew more than I did and was better at life than I was so there must be something I was doing wrong I'm sure. He leaned over started rubbing my shoulder lightly as if he was beginning a stages of grooming. I shrugged him off cuz I was sad and confused. And you wrapped his arms around me he said you have to understand something if you're going to live here you have to offer something. If you're not going to work and I have to take care of you you have to offer me something. You have to be useful in some way. So I thought to myself well I guess if I do want a real nice place to live I do have to offer something so I did I offered the exchange sex for a place to live. The first form of prostitution I ever came across. I learned the most valuable lesson that day. No one's ever going to take care of me because they care about me. They will take care of me and exchange for sex and if I sacrifice my freedom. What I thought was the beginning to a new level in life I found was only another prison.

CHAPTER 4

After weeks of depression and performing my domestic duties.
I finally planned my escape. He goes to work everyday and instead of drinking
my day away I decided one night that I was going to pack up everything
I had and get out as fast as I could. And never look back. Fortunately my
plan worked I got my three tubs of clothes and memories from childhood
that I drug with me everywhere I went . I was finally out of there and went
straight back to the club so that I could have a decent life and freedom the
kind that I had worked so hard for at this point. Not knowing where to go
but wanting to stay in Columbus closer to where I worked I found a hotel I
could stay in for a little while. So I stayed there for about 2 months deciding
what to do next. I found an apartment complex gone apartment and moved
in. I was finally free at last I had my own place again taking care of myself
and no one could control my every move or dictate my life. Back to my safe
place with the club being my survival.

Somehow I learned how to stay sober while I was at work. I knew it
was the difference between having a job versus not having a job so I talked
it out and I so weird up while I was at work. And then I did all my binge
drinking at night and on my days off. That helped a lot! So what do I do
now what's my next move I'm definitely not moving in with another man
that's for sure that was right up there next to a death sentence. No freedom
made into a sex slave. No thank you I am not interested! So what was my
next move I started working 4 days a week just cuz I had nothing better to
do. Thursday Friday Saturday and Sunday night. I was bringing in all this
money had nowhere to put it nothing to do with it. I learned my lesson about
not bringing people into my home because they would either rob me, steal

for me or bring drugs in and I didn't want any of that so I decided keeping my home private and safe was the best option. Now that I'm not dating because that was spoiled by a fantasy that turned out to be a prison I didn't know what to do next. One day I drove by a new build complex where they were building new homes in my community I'd seen them before but now I wondered if I could build one. So at 19 years old I stopped in the model complex and ask them if I could build a house. They said I need to find a mortgage company but I didn't know anything about what that was. So they gave me a phone number to somebody who could help me get a mortgage so I can build a house. I contacted the mortgage company before I knew it I was under contract to build a new home! How exciting I could now afford to build a new home! And it would be my home and I got to design it anyway I want it! Wow my dreams really are coming true now I'm building a home! My home! Month after month they started building my home I think it took about 7 months total it was exciting exhilarating I didn't know what to think! I was so excited I took pictures when I put the two before's up and then more pictures when the wood was being put up in the roof wow every month I saw more and more things happening and they were building my house it was so amazing and I got to design it too. I went to their model home place and I got to pick out the countertop the color of the floor color of the walls the wood trim I got to pick out everything it was so amazing and I picked out the layout to the actual house! How amazing is that! I was so excited I can't say that enough I was just so excited.

It was December 2004 has 20 years old seeing the girls are flying up to Manhattan a sister club of where I worked. They asked if I wanted to go with them, go work at a club up north in New York city. I was nervous with invitation, but I was always up for a good adventure and I accepted. We have plans to stay there for one week got a room for all three of us. So we flew up north month of December excited to for a new adventure I'm working in Manhattan New york, wow! The flights were overwhelming as there was everything was so fast paced airports were overwhelming because everyone seemed like they knew where they were going and I just felt like I was like a lost puppy just being banged around and following the other girls hoping they knew what to do. We got a taxi cab from the airport to our hotel and then the next night we showed up at the club. They were waiting for us! So we dressed ourselves gotten our best outfits and hit the floor. It was a three-story club the biggest club I never seen. The stage is a lot smaller than I was used to and most of the attraction was everywhere else in stage had one girl on it and there was very little attention. There were two large red staircases they went from one floor to the next .

I felt confident comfortable and ready to have the time of my life. I went out there with my still pixie haircut from my fantasized life of being a real estate agent that clearly didn't work out. My usual black and white tight halter dress that came down to the bottom of my buttocks. I did so well and Columbus that I thought everything would be faster and easier here! After all I'm in the big city. But for some reason when I went out onto the floor no one would look at me. All these real fancy businessmen and there are three tiered suits slipped back hair and fine leather wallets. No one wanted to look at me. So I just walk out sit on someone's lap try to start small talk and they would quickly tell me they were waiting on someone after that happening a few times I thought well maybe I need to just take off my clothes. So that was my next step I'll just stand right in front of them and ask if they want collapse dance. So I did and even when I did that the patrons would tell me no finally one guy after telling me no three times gave me $20 just to leave them alone. Gosh I was so confused what am I missing. It wasn't like this back home people were fighting to get my attention usually. Throwing money at me trying to get me to look their way. What was I doing wrong? So I sat in the back by myself and I just watched I looked around thinking what's different about them than me. Then it came to me these girls had big fake boobs and long hair most of them blonde hair but all of them had long hair. That was the difference big boobs and long hair. Apparently my b cut natural breast and my short pixie hair modeling Halle Berry wasn't the look they were going for in the big city. I swallowed my pride and I went to the other girls and told them I wasn't going to make it in a big city I didn't have what it takes. They seem confused considering I was one of the top hustlers back home. I didn't have time to explain I just wanted to let them know that I was going to go back to the hotel get my things and fly back home early because time is money and I don't have time to waste here cuz I'm losing money. I followed up by telling the manager that for some reason I wasn't making it in the big city and I needed to go back home they were empathetic just wish me luck. So that night terrified I switched my flight jumped on a plane and was back in Columbus Ohio in no time. I was overwhelmed anxious humiliated confused. Never felt so ugly in my entire life. It's one thing if someone says they don't have time, they're sitting with someone else but when someone blatantly pays you to go away when you're not wearing any clothes…that was a rejection I had never felt before. There were times I would take it personal because obviously everyone wants to feel accepted or wanted in some way but this took rejection to a whole other level there was nothing I could say or do to convince this person I was Worthy of anything. And they were willing to give me money to leave them alone. I cried I cussed and then I looked up plastic surgeons. I booked a surgery in January to double my cup size and found a hair extension artist to make my hair longer again. I was going to fit the mold I was going to make it in the big cities.

Some people think that when you're attractive you don't know what rejection is but I'll be the first to tell you when you get rejected with your clothes off so many times a week and so many times and one night let me tell you you learn how to deal with rejection in a way that no one else could. That was the year I mastered weathering rejection with a smile. I couldn't control them I couldn't control what they wanted letting go of my pride and the desire to be wanted. And someone told me no look the other way or handed me money to leave them alone I'd take that money and I'd walk away with a smile cuz I tried. That was the most important thing that I learned is if you don't try you only have one option. But if you do try and fail at least you have two options you either have a the option to achieve or the option to fail. And even if I did fail I can learn from it and figure out how to get up and try it again. And that's what I was really good at really I didn't even know anything about failure I just knew how to try a million times until I figured it out. Barrier was never really in my vocabulary anyway I didn't know how to fail only way thing I knew how to do in life was to keep trying until something worked!

6 months later I was moving into my brand new belt 1600 ft house had a new look with long Sandy brown hair with caramel highlights and a size d cup in the bust. I topped it off with working out and getting my waist set size down to five. I had arrived I had a home that was mine all the food I could want he hot water as beautiful the best fitness I'd ever been in living on the fancy end of town which I could only dream of when I was a little girl. I was moving up the ladder.! So I decided to do more traveling now that I had my home in Columbus I started traveling to different cities Chicago, Las vegas, dallas, tampa, atlanta! I figured out how to make it in the big cities and let me tell you I was making it it was a beautiful thing I was now officially in the major leagues of the adult entertainment world sky was the limit in so many areas. I felt like I was on top of the world! I flew out to Vegas a second time after I turned 21. You had to be 21 to work in Vegas because you needed an entertainment license to work out there. Second time I flew out there I stayed with a man that I met through mutual contact. He had a normal looking house live like a bachelor mid-30s. Working out there was fun but he offered to take me on a trip to the Grand canyon. I never been to the Grand canyon and I wanted a new adventure anyway so I took him up on his offer. We took the weekend went out to the Grand canyon and had a blast. I got plenty of beautiful shots out there some of them clothes some of them without clothes you know I had to live out my fantasy somehow. What an exploration and I got to drink as much as I want. So many beautiful sites out there you can't make it up.

I'll never forget the trip back to the airport in Las vegas. We had finished our fun excursion at the Grand canyon took lots of pictures how to unbelievable alcohol and sex. Finally making our way back to the airport my friend Rob decided to give me some advice. He told me I don't think you're going to like what I have to say but someone needs to tell you, you need help you need therapy you need help. I'm telling you this cuz someone cared about me enough to tell me this. I was completely irate who did he think he was talking to I had everything any person could ever dream of looks a big house all the money I could think of as well taken care of and impeccable shape and this man thinks I need help I don't know what kind of crack cocaine he's on, but he was wrong and I let him have it ice cream and yelled at him I hit him in the arm a couple times just to make a point that he was wrong I did not need help I was perfect just the way I was and he was the one that was crazy! I screamed and shouted at him until we he dropped me off at the airport I got out with a vengeance. I can't believe this mother f***** would say something like that to me. Who does he think he is anyway! So I flew back home four hour flight from Las Vegas back to Columbus Ohio pounding the liquor in the air the whole time. Somehow I made it back home. My adventure my triumph was over. I finally reached the top of adult entertainment I finally was able to make it in any City I wanted anytime I wanted in conquering Las Vegas was the last on my checklist. I was the best I am the best I have finally proven that I am valuable and I have something to offer. And I can go anywhere and have anything I want anytime! 21 years old and I finally made it to the very top of what I thought was success. But little did I know right around the corner was my huge crash.

CHAPTER 5

FROM THE TO TO THE BOTTOM

I laid on my back in front of my perfect gas lit fireplace in my beautiful new built home. I was a success. I had finally reached the top of my industry I've conquered everything I had wanted and needed and I proved to myself that I can make it with the best in the major leagues! I felt like there is nothing I couldn't do nowhere I could couldn't go and nothing I couldn't have. So why having all of this accomplished a 21 years old did I feel so sad, so alone so unwanted so invaluable. Why was I laying there with a glass of white zinfandel a Black and mild cigar in my right hand laying in front of the fireplace considering suicide. Why did I want to die? This is the most confusing place I've ever been. I finally set out on everything I wanted to do I'm well taken care of more beautiful and More in shape than I could ever imagine and I just want to kill myself. The loneliness was so deep inside of me I could barely breathe and when I did it was just inhale the tobacco for my cigar. The tears rolled down my face. There is no sobbing energy left. I was just so incredibly sad alone and empty. There is a void inside of me bigger then the shell of my body and no one can see it or hear it. The only thing that lighten the load is when I went into the club and felt wanted for the hours I was there then I left feeling more empty than I went in. And now I've conquered everything and I feel like dying more than ever. What was I to do? Where do you go from here once you reach the top? There's nowhere left to go you're at the top and you're just by your fucking self.

For 2 weeks I laid in that same spot in front of my fireplace
with a cigar in one hand and a glass of wine in the other. Drinking bottle
after bottle until I pass out. On the weekends I'd go into work perform at my
best and felt wanted and valued, at least for the 12 hours I would I worked.

So what's left what do I do now? Maybe that man in Vegas was right. So
I found myself contemplating do I kill myself or call a therapist. Well didn't
take long to make that decision. Considering my void and black hole in my
soul was growing deeper and deeper. So I started calling therapist nearby.
Company after company told me they weren't taking any new clients and they
were fullp. So I decided to start leaving messages on those individual therapists voicemails. I didn't at first cuz I wanted someone to talk to on the other
line but after 2 days of striking out and not finding the therapist to take on a
new client I decided to start leaving messages. So 4 days of calling multiple
therapists in Columbus Ohio leaving messages after messages hoping that
someone would call me back and say they had an opening. The following
week I got a call from a lady that said she was taking on new clients. Her
schedule sounded open and I was so desperate I would take anything. So
the only therapist available I took the moment she said she had an opening.
I could when I walked in it was quiet awkward building and the upstairs
unit. The paint looked old the books on the shelf were very retired and the
shelf itself looked like it was donated. Everything kind of had an echo as if
the whole place was slightly hollow, but I had nothing to lose at this point
and everything to gain. The lady came out she had shoulder length reddish
brown hair maybe in her 60s. She had a soft voice and was tall and slender
with natural colored clothes khaki pants and a cream-colored sweater. It was
winter so of course we were both dressed warm. She had me fill out some
paperwork and then called me back to her office when I finished. There is
no receptionist so obviously she was working on her own. She asked me
why I was there and what brings me in. I told her I don't really know but I
just needed help, I went to Vegas worked a little met someone and they told
me I needed help and I feel so sad and empty so I decided to get help. She
empathized responded compassionately to how I felt and we made some

goals together about how I could improve my life or what that would even look like. And so the journey began.

The journey to building self-esteem and so forth, the journey to digging through my past and grieving the family that I never had, learning how what feelings were how to express them appropriately and how to stop lashing out violently at other people. I have to admit that was very helpful I didn't want to be violent whenever I lash out at someone and hit them I didn't mean to it was like my body took over me I couldn't control it sometimes it would happen at customers at work sometimes it would happen if I was out and a girl approached me the wrong way sometimes it would happen with a significant other that I was dating for a two or three week time Sprint frame the defended me and the only way I knew how to respond was to throw a punch. I hated that part about me but it's not like I knew any other way to communicate stop or I'm upset. The throwing punches was all I knew how to do violence was something that just took over my body and I didn't want to be violent even my boss warned me to stop being violent because if I continued he'd have to fire me. So that was my biggest thing is I just didn't want to be violent anymore. But didn't know how to stop.

That year so many beautiful things happen for me I was able to build up who I was as a person and not base my value on who wanted me, how much money I made that night or how attractive I felt. I actually started feeling valuable as a person. I started reading these books she gave me there was so much information in the books that she gave me. So much insight about building self-esteem and self-worth it was incredible. Then on top of that learning how to articulate my feelings and express myself with words and not violence. I learned how to store it in my thinking was I thought everyone was out to get me I thought everyone wanted to hurt me. Turns out that's not the reality at all whenever anyone got upset with me all the sudden I learned how to have compassion for them because I knew that lashing out is it trying to accomplish one thing we all just want to feel better. When we're hurting and we're in pain we just want to feel better for some people it's lashing out physically, other people with lashing out verbally, some people cut, cry, or even have sex or drink. We're all just wounded people walking around wanting to feel better and everything we do we're just trying to feel better and some of it's just don't have healthy ways to do that because nobody ever taught us. Thank God I met this woman it was like she was a mother to me. She taught me about myself how to be a lady how to conduct myself how to take care of myself. One of the most valuable things she taught me was get up in the morning no matter how you feel put your makeup on take a shower take care of yourself. And then go throughout the rest of your day. So that's when I learned how to take care of myself first thing in the morning no matter how I felt no matter what I was thinking no matter what the situation was I just had to take care of myself and go through my day. I've been doing that ever since and that was the best advice starting out that she could ever give me. Age 22 was awesome I actually became a woman put away my white trailer trash attitude I was able to conduct myself with some respect. You can't do that unless someone teaches you so thank God this woman taught me how to conduct myself in society. It was hard cuz working a strip club you can say and do anything you want basically you're only getting in trouble if somebody gets hurt or if you're breaking the law. So learning any kind of standard of professional conduct without the door. But now I'm learning how to be a normal human being communicate with words and not violence, learn how to trust other people and what trust even looks like, what trustworthiness is, what it means to care and to be respected, to learn my feelings and what they mean and what they look like and being willing to humble myself and question my reality and my perception. This lady was a PhD in psychology and let me tell you she gave me my PhD in psychology just by teaching me what she knows she was my miracle! Another sign of hope that everything was going to be okay at some point. But at least for now I started to feel better and I didn't want to kill myself anymore that was a relief.

Balance meditation and peace was the focus we always came back to in therapy. A balance with my time balance with money balance and relationships balance in life. Meditating in the morning even if it was just for

10 minutes is how I learned to start my day. If I centered and focused my day on inner peace and balance the day usually would go well. If I forgot or just neglected it life got out of hand pretty quickly. I saw the therapist three times a week for at least 2 years. Working through my violent tendencies, low self-esteem, distorted thinking, black and white thinking, inferiority complex. Need I go on? I never thought that these first 5 years in therapy would have propelled me into the amazing life I have now. At the time it was just pain tears struggle and lots of feelings that I didn't know how to handle or what to do with most of the time. But I learned, I learned this too shall pass, the world doesn't revolve around me, we're all fighting a battle, and I'm not alone as long as I believe in god. With all the balancing acts I was playing in my life I started to feel emotional emotionally stable after about 3 years. It is 2006 my life had settled down for the most part and then the recession hit. The mortgage industry crashed traumatically and all the sudden my income was significantly affected. All the quote on quote sales were down 60% and I was devastated feeling the financial loss and the emotional instability that went with it I panicked. But after asking around for about 6 months I finally decided to go to nursing school. It was my only hope for some kind of stability again!

Feeling like I was selling my soul to the devil on a daily basis the timing was appropriate. As I started realizing my emotions jumbled up between taking my clothes off for money, and my new developed self-worth going into a new field of study was very timely. I went to college for nursing only obtaining my LPN degree. I wanted to go my RN but unfortunately throughout my whole training I was drunk. And if the interview to go into the RN portion the school clarified that I was in the bottom 5% of my class and I didn't stand a chance to get in unless half of the students that applied for the RN program decided to drop out. So they basically let me know pretty clearly that RN portion was not an option for me. I know I was intelligent I knew I have what it took and the drive, but I also knew I was a drunk and really didn't want to go to RN portion anyway I barely survived the lpn! After 2 years of drunken episodes after class gaining 30 lb and still hoping to make an income on the weekends regardless I survived and past my nursing boards.

After working throughout the whole city of Dayton and Columbus in the strip clubs I felt that my reputation had been quite a bit tainted! So I thought the best option would be to relocate out of ohio. On spring break I found Charleston South Carolina to be my next big move. Leaving my therapist is one of the most difficult things I've ever done she was only person that ever had anything to offer me, like a mother like a mentor like anybody. She stuck by me even when I canceled appointments, yelled at her, gave her the cold shoulder treatment, accused her of manipulating me I gave her such a hard time because I was just so jaded by the world using me and feeling nobody cared. But she did. This therapist was the first person that cared so much about me and didn't give up on me even when I did multiple times. It was so hard for me to leave her that I never even went to the goodbye session I canceled it and left town. I understand when someone cares so much about another person they can't say goodbye. Yes the mature thing is to say goodbye but if you don't have that maturity leaving unannounced with no communication is the only skill I had at the time. I loved her like a mother, like a grandmother like a therapist. Still to this day I never said goodbye, I guess maybe it's cuz I don't want to choose the best thing that ever happened to me.

So here I go sold everything out of my house had a property management company take over my house to run it out, I piled my miniature black and white terrier dog that never stopped barking, my black cat named Savannah and my white and gray cat named princess, and everything I could fit in my Silver Toyota solara convertible. Jumped on 71 and headed south to Charleston South Carolina.

CHAPTER 6

LEARNING TO SHUT UP

I went straight to what I knew best sleeping in a hotel when I had nowhere else to go. I found a motel that would allow three pets. You can only imagine what kind of motel that would be. But they took us in and I stayed there for about a month, well I searched the area trying to find the side of town I liked, the area I like, and the apartments that were suitable. I landed on the north side of the coast which was very classy money driven area, what I was used to really. For the first few months I was there I continued dancing. Tried a few clubs in the area and then went outside at the area, trying to play it safe so I didn't run into anyone I might work with in the future in the medical field. But I was still drunk. While I was waiting on my nursing license to transfer from one state to the next I hung out with the retired folks drinking all through the week and then on the weekends I'd make my way to the club to make a living. I did that for about 6 months finally my LPN license transferred, and I set up my first job interview. Oh was I excited working in a doctor's office. I went into the interview I always nailed interviews because of my people skills, so that was never a concern but I went into the interview with a horrible hangover. I remember thinking I have no idea how I'm going to work 5 days a week and get up in the morning 5 days a week as a drunk. I've been a drunk since 22 to 25 at this point. So it's not long but it's long enough to realize I can't function without alcohol. So I decided it was time to go back into therapy found a local therapist and she's the one that I had to get sober. I told her alcohol wasn't the problem I was I needed help just functioning when I wasn't drinking cuz the drinking was what helped everything. Oh the insanity even saying it out loud right now it sounds so crazy. But when she told me she wouldn't help me unless I got sober, I knew I had no choice. A therapist was only person that was able to help me in my entire adulthood, so I wasn't going to lose that now. So I decided to try what she suggested get a sponsor go to meetings work the steps. She reassured me that I tried it for 6 months and I'm not satisfied with the results she won't fully refund my misery. It really wasn't much of a task to agree to cuz I really was miserable and I was trying to figure out how to have a better life even with self-esteem and self-worth I was still drunk. Oh my god!

So I took the job at the doctor's office, and sobered up at the same time. It was quite a difference being going from being the center of everyone's attention to a doctor being the center of everyone's attention. I was so confused half the time because everyone was constantly begging for his approval and got their feelings hurt when he didn't approve and competed with the other staff for his attention. I didn't understand what all the commotion was about honestly. He was a doctor yes but he wasn't God but everyone sure treated him that way. I didn't give him that kind of attention because he was just another person like the rest of us, honestly he was scary though. When he yelled at me for making a mistake I did what I do best, I froze then I'd get yelled at for freezing just like the military. What a confusing way to get sober let me tell you. The only the real things I learned there is to keep my mouth shut, because I had a really bad mouth and I knew how to give someone my opinion real quickly. So if this office I learned two things one had to keep my mouth shut and two had to be a worker among workers. I was so used to the spotlight and being someone important and significant in the strip club that being a part of a community and just like everybody else I felt like a lost puppy dog. I was supposed to do what everyone else does and blend in as if I was another schmuck there to get a paycheck. Thank God everyone noticed I was pretty I at least I at least had that going for me. But other than my appearance I was fully clothed and I never felt so vulnerable in my life.

It's crazy but when I started wearing clothes and being around people for the first time I felt like people were looking at me and not my body. I felt so exposed emotionally. At least if someone was looking at me naked I knew what they were thinking, or at least what level we were on. In exchange. But when I wore clothes all the sudden people looked in my eyes, that was the most vulnerable scariest thing I had ever experienced is someone actually looking at me. My old childhood I didn't matter to anybody I was lucky if someone noticed me usually it was because of my appearance. And then from 18 to 25 when people looked at me all they saw was my body some sexual being that was going to make them feel good. But now I'm a nurse. People look in my eyes they respect me and they don't know anything about me. That was the other thing I noticed after becoming a nurse. All the sudden people respected me just for my label. Part of that made me so angry because I wanted to be respected for who I was, but it's not like I ever experienced that anyway so what's the big deal and now people respect me because I have a different profession all of a sudden that's what made me angry cuz I was still the same person it's just a job. But I just swallow my pride of wanting to feel valuable for who I was and just be okay with the fact that people respected me because I work in a different profession now. It was a lot easier to talk to people because everyone seemed to want to open up to me. I don't know why it surprised me so much but before I was shunned you know I was a stripper I dress provocatively I had made sexual inappropriate comments on a regular basis even outside the club because I my reality was so tainted by what I worked with. But I had to learn how to talk like a lady I had to learn how to blend in I had to not mouth off because I was in a bad mood. God holding my tongue was such a hurdle the biggest hurdle really is learning how to keep my mouth shut I got fired from two or three jobs before I actually realized it was my mouth that was getting me fired. Apparently you're not supposed to tell off your boss in front of government inspections, but I'm a late learner in that regard. The struggle was real I would go through episodes of feeling like I was powerful and in charge being a nurse and then once I'd lose that job because of my ego and foul mouth, the humility would start all over again and then I would be able to shut my mouth again and treat people like human beings and not like they were beneath me. I didn't mean to get that way it just I'd boss people around for so long being a stripper it was so hard to be nice. My soul was still really hardened from all the abuse that I've endured over my lifetime but at least I was learning how to handle it better. Plus with sobriety I at least had some good outlets my sponsor some friends. But even then I was so self absorbed I left little room to hear about anybody else's day or care how someone else is doing it was a long process it's still a long process but the more good habits I make today the better habits I have tomorrow. And being of service. Whenever I get out of the mentality of being of service whether it's to my job or friends I tend to screw things up pretty bad when I make everything about me. So I'm still slowly learning.

After spoiling the third job in nursing God finally sent me to a family that I couldn't ruin. They spoke a complete other language and barely knew any english. Talk about God teaching me how to shut up even if I tried to talk no one would understand what I was saying. So in a strange way working with a family that didn't know English was the best thing that could ever happen to me. So when I said something that was inappropriate or out of line nobody understood it and I had a chance to realize what I said was inappropriate or out of line. What a beautiful gift to be able to make mistakes and forgiven on the spot. So I worked at job for about a year and I learned their language I and by doing that I learned how to speak appropriately because we talked on a need to know basis and nursing. I experience compassion for the first time seeing what it was like from an immigrant's perspective in the United states. I was humbled in ways that year that I had never been humbled before. Even though I struggled as a child my adult years took away a lot of humility replaced it all with ego and pride. So even though it was difficult some days even invariable learning compassion and humility all over again with such a gift.

CHAPTER 7

I'LL KILL YOU IF YOU EVER LEAVE

Finally after a year I'm getting sober from alcohol I had enough self-restrained to keep my mouth shut and my hands off people, and I learned at least how to take orders from other people. I hadn't quite developed the scale of working well with others, but if you told me what to do I would shut my mouth and do it. That at least kept me employable.

I came up with a regular routine of meetings, work schedule and getting all this stress out at the gym. The next thing I know David, a charming, good looking man that just moved to Charleston from New York started following me around meetings. I was naive thinking we just happened to go to the same places at the same time. But little did I know the stocking began. He was about 90 days sober had a great spiel about why he moved to South Carolina to be with family and a charisma they could turn the pants off anybody. Everyone around me was so fixated on him and everything he had to say. Of course with enough time and attention I decided to let him take me on a date. But somehow one date at church would turn into a 3-day adventure. I started to feel suffocated and would ask for space. He would listen for one day maybe too if I was lucky but then the phone calls would start, the first time it happened he called seven times in the first day and when I didn't pick up he finally showed up at my house at 6:00 p.m. . Thinking in my mind I was so irresistible you couldn't stay away from me I found myself flattered. Here is this intoxicating man that can't get enough of me, this must be love. I even asked my sponsor at one point what her opinion was on all the phone calls and showing up at my door. Her response was it's a sign from God that he was supposed to be in my life. Oh my how little did either of us know. It was a sign from God letting me know he's trying to control me and Rob his hands around my throat and suffocate me to death. But I wasn't there yet I was too busy being mesmerized by the fact that this man couldn't get enough of me! After a year of tug of , pushing him away him showing up on my doorstep, following me to meetings on the other side of town, and cock blocking any man that ever even looked at me, I finally caved. I was not going to get rid of this man and nobody else would approach me at this point because he had a way of making his way in front of anybody that was around me. So I finally submitted we moved in together and got engaged to be married. It was very confusing time for me. I was 26 had a great career, sober a year and a half from alcohol and then a toxic relationship with someone that I didn't even like, and now I'm engaged to be married. To top it off so many women in the program admired our relationship and me in my recovery. So I was even more confused because everyone was looking up to me and are engagement and I was absolutely miserable.

So that year in 2011 I had one year of sobriety from alcohol and stumbled into a 12-step program for codependency. Apparently it was codependency, control, people pleasing, and unmet needs that made my life so unmanageable and so miserable. All of which I had the resources to change myself because it was my behavior that needed the help. Still frustrated anger spilling out and spurts I continued in that program making progress in the relationship. After a couple months in the program I decided to postpone the engagement and then later ended the relationship. As I learned more of how to love with no strings attached, except people for who they are and not try to change them, in focus on my attitude and how to have a healthy grateful perspective in life; I realized within 6 months that I can accept someone for who they are but I don't have to like them. And in this case I don't have to marry them either! I can love with no strings attached but not tolerate abuse, I don't have to accept unacceptable behavior what a revolution. And my attitude is more grateful and healthier when I take care of my own needs give myself the love,appreciation, rest, time, and support that I need. When I take care of myself all the sudden I'm able to have compassion for myself and other people. That was a whole new level of life that I never experienced self-compassion wow. Even though it was such a struggle and so much anger before I found the codependency program it was the best thing that ever happened to me because all the sudden I knew how to take care of myself and find freedom and happiness within me.

CHAPTER 8

WE CANNOT GRADUATE YOU

A dream of mine was always to join the military. For whatever reason I never followed through I would go to the different stations air force, marines, Navy, Coast guard. But I never signed up because I was so afraid of the commitment. Now I'm free of relationships and with my newfound sobriety I felt like I was able to take orders like a soldier. Having had a rough life to begin with being strong with second nature to me. So I decided to go into the coast guard. So I memorized all the things I needed to memorize, and gotten really good shape. I was sent off to New Jersey for boot camp. Scared and excited a whole gang of emotions. But the one thing I knew learned how to do was to shut up and listen and do as I'm told. So that's what I did. But all the while I was there my boots were too big and they rubbed my feet and I started getting blisters but I was too afraid to ask for what I needed and so my running suffered my performance suffered, I suffered. Between being yelled at lack of sleep no self-care, I started getting sick. My body was starting to shut down. So when I went to the nurses station they gave me Robitussin oh I found my small percentage of alcohol that was going to see me through. If you go to the nurses station they'll give you as much as you want. So that's what I did for the following two weeks. Somehow I found myself drunk while in boot camp off of Robitussin laughing inappropriately not able to keep up with my classmates but my blisters weren't in pain anymore and I didn't care if I was the last in line. I tried so hard to behave but the comfort of that Robitussin was just enough to keep me going. Finally in the last week of boot camp I received amazing support and letters from my sister's and family and brother. It was more love than I've ever experienced. Then one evening I got a letter from my little sister. My sister who was 26 at the time was diagnosed with stage 4 adrenal cancer. She communicated this to me in the letter and I completely fell apart when I read it. The sergeant made me read it with everyone standing around so I went from moments of Joy hearing from my little sister to moments of terror hearing about or possible death sentence. After that for days I couldn't function and they pulled me out. Just keep going, just keep going, just keep going it was the only words I could repeat to myself because that's the only thing I knew how to do. 2 days before the graduation they notified me that I was not going to graduate with the others. I knew between my Robitussin medicating, my emotional outburst from the letter from my sister, and my deep despair a feeling abused throughout boot camp there is no way I could continue in no way I was going to fight for a position there. I submitted and cried the whole ride back from South Carolina from to South Carolina. What do I do? How do I function? Is my sister going to die? I'm so glad I'm out of there! The military is not for me.

After careful consideration I decided to move back to Springfield ohio. I wanted to be close to sister I also wanted to help if I could. Within 6 months I moved back to Ohio and got a place with my brother we were roommates. We initially tried having family get togethers all of us playing pretend. But that wore off quickly and the the groups and the family started separating and as much as we wanted to support our sister I know I was the main one pushed away. They told me be Mary not Martha. In the Bible Mary was the one that sat down and spent time with Jesus and Martha was the one washing dishes and trying to get things done instead of enjoying his company. So I was advised to be Mary not Martha. So that's what I did I tried to just spend time with my sister enjoy your company. I tried to do that for a couple months but shortly after the expectations began what you're doing isn't good enough you are not good enough you need to do more we want more more more! More money more effort more time more responsibility. I knew there was nothing I could do to change the outcome of her cancer. I knew no amount of money that I handed them was going to make it go away. And I knew the time I had with her was all either of us had to offer. But no one else could see it that way. I had cleaned out my savings account which wasn't much a little over $3,000 at that point trying to help out with medications transportation gas insurance. I know everyone was chipping in but it was nothing was enough. So after a while I just decided to quit trying. I didn't have any money left to give so I stopped giving it. The more I tried to do to help out around the house angry or I would get because I knew this wasn't valuable to me what was valuable was the time that I had left with her. So I would grow angry as I did chores or move things around in the closet or pick things up off the floor. Cuz that's not what I was there to do I was happy to do it but I just wanted to spend time with my sister. Real time with someone I love, that didn't see any value in that. I found myself not wanting to go over after a while around that same time frame I quit getting invitations to come over. It's funny how the energy you put out is the energy that you get. So even though it was difficult not being around I was so thankful that I could use my time for people that wanted my time and not something I had to offer. I can invest in relationships that were investing in the relationship and not just wanted something from me. I realized that someone with cancer may have a very different perspective and I can totally respect that but I'm only writing for my perspective that's all I have. I love my sister more than life itself but I realized at that time we had two different things that were priority. And all I knew that my priority was to spend time with my sister valuable loving pleasant time. Time I'll never get back.

After a period of time I was cut off from most communication from my sister Angela. Device from my family was to just give her space is that's what she needed as she's going through her own healing. Fortunately I could see on Facebook she was climbing mountains, jumping out of airplanes skydiving, imposing a magazines to uplift people with cancer. I was so happy to see that she was continuing to live life and to its fullest and have the experiences that she wanted while she was here. I o

I on the other hand started dating again living in Springfield that was almost a hobby of mine. I realize that my one Downfall with every relationship I had is I always slept with a person before I knew them. But I didn't know how to not sleep with them I discovered a group for people with addictive sexual compulsions. I had a long list of that! I could go for weeks on end with nothing and then I would binge just like a alcoholic would except I would do it with sex excursions. I knew this is an issue for me and part of the issue why I kept getting into relationships with people I don't even like. Not knowing how to solve the issued I stumbled into another 12-step recovery program that dealt with specific sex problems.

CHAPTER 9

SEXACAPADE

Knowing that I continue getting into unsafe relationships I realized I needed a guide in this area. I started participating in these groups and met my first husband quickly he was uncomfortable with the idea of me participating in his groups because they're predominantly men, so I decided to stop going and focus on my marriage. Neither one of us were going to groups anymore but God help both of us we needed it. The next thing I knew we were pregnant and so excited! It would be the first grandchild on both sides of our family holy cow! For 5 months we got the crib ready the bedroom ready painted the walls purple and lime green the colors of a fairy it was so exciting and so amazing and my sister was still alive so she would get to meet her niece. Her cancer continued to grow and 5 months into my pregnancy I found out the child was down syndrome. Not ready to take on a special needs child with a broken but strong heart I decided to have an abortion. I was not prepared to take on a child that needed so much assistance even if I did have so much love to offer. Coming from a religious background it was so hard to communicate this is my family did not share similar reviews or perspective. It was the most daunting got wrenching decision I've ever had to make especially at such a fragile time in my life as well. Here I am my sister's passing away from cancer given one more year to live, I have the first possible grandchild growing inside of me, and I decide not to have it after it's been announced clothes coming out my ears from friends and families gifts for the baby. It was so devastating for everybody. But I knew the responsibility that goes with it and I was not willing to take that on, even if I could I wasn't willing to. God that was a hard decision such a hard decision to make me and my husband were the only two on board I still carry Shane to this day I think anybody that's ever had an abortion does but the timing of this and then after the announcement and everything was just devastating to everybody.

After feeling blackballed from the family partially because I wasn't fulfilling my sisterly cancer duties, and then a boarding the possible first grandchild in the family I somehow managed with my codependency program to continue living a life that created peace and happiness for myself. My husband and I went on vacation to the beach, horseback riding, stayed in recovery programs, and enjoyed our evening TV routine. I continued living a full life and making choices that brought me peace and happiness every day. All the while my sex addiction continued to Fester. I was pushing my husband to do more and more risky behavior. Some things we're in places we could have been caught, other things were lots of role-playing dominatrix and I got to pull some of my pole dancing days back into my life again. He was my only audience that got it felt good to be back on a pole. I miss feeling sexy I miss feeling wanted I missed pretending that I was a man's greatest reward. There's so much power that came with sex addictionp. Really that's what I miss more than anything I miss the power that's what it was I missed the power so I used my power over my husband pushing him in so many unfair ways. Asking him to do things that were not legal, forcing him to sleep with me when he didn't want to, I'm using all the power of seduction I could to win his favor whenever there was a dispute between me and his family. There was a lot of control issues in his family and I saw it even before we were married but I thought I could fix it I thought I would win. But love isn't about winning love is about wanting someone else to be happy. But somehow I missed all of that when I lost my sex program. When I flush that out the door all of the sudden I was the only one that mattered, my fantasies had to be fulfilled, and nobody else better stand in my way.

Like any great sex adventure it almost come to an end at some point. My end came in February when my sister died. I was living in my own world my own Fantasyland with my husband thinking I'd conquered it all, and then weeks came where her decline came faster and faster until she was bedridden for 2 weeks. One week a week and a half in the hospital and then the last 4 days at home. My little sister and the one I raised died at 28 of adrenal cancer. Everyone has their opinion of what causes cancer, but what I learned in that year has carried me to this very day. Stress and trauma kills people and so many different ways my two sisters and one brother and myself all come from a very traumatic background like many. Some people deal with trauma through drugs, some deal with it through alcohol, some deal with it through sex, some people kill themselves because they can't deal with it, and sometimes the trauma that happens to them and their childhood continues into their adult life and their body can't handle it., Catches up with us at some point in life and if we're not given the proper skills to deal with it trauma kills us some of us earlier in life some of us later in life some of us by our own making. But trauma kills people everyday all day long. Sometimes it's in the form of alcoholism, drug addiction suicide, relationships, codependency, ocd, overeating, cancer. Trauma equals death.

All all the sudden life came to a complete halt my marriage my sex excursions my goals purpose so I can all just disappeared in one day I joined a grief group cuz I didn't know what else to do I couldn't stop crying I could barely get out of bed I couldn't hold a Job I was in my LPN to RN school and I had to drop out because of panic attacks. My whole world completely crashed and my husband left me. 2015 was the worst year I'd ever experienced and I had no idea how to recover all the sudden nothing mattered to me anymore but then somehow everything mattered at the same time it didn't make any sense.

The process of moving out was terrible. My husband moved in with his parents house temporarily while I found employment and tried to get myself together. They asked me daily, every time I left the house they would enter the house and move furniture around. This left me feeling violated afraid confused and alone. Not feeling safe on a daily basis in a place that you once called home is devastating, and realizing you can't do anything about it it's just defeating. So day after day I weathered the move furniture pictures moving on and off the walls,. Periodically watching them enter the house as I was leaving. It was very bizarre. But finally after a couple months I landed a job and a place to stay and move out. I finally was settled long enough in the apartment to feel again. Up until that point I had been numb with fear and disillusion. Once I was in the apartment the meltdown began. I was working third shift nursing home health job. I was able to hold it together long enough for a 10-hour shift and then when I got home I would fall apart all over again NyQuil and sleeping medication was the only way I got through some days. The other days I was full of rage and would go to the gym exercise as much as I could sometimes at home turn furniture over just to get the anger out. Still going to therapy I was able to communicate properly some of my emotions most of it being grief and loss.

CHAPTER 10

A REASON TO LIVE

Day after day after meltdown panic attack raging and excessive grief. I finally came to a point where I was ready to be done. All my anger had just become numbness my fear had become defeat in my confusion had become the acceptance of not knowing what I'm doing in life and I'm going nowhere. The day came where I decided with a cocktail of anxiety medication sleeping medication and pain medication I might have just the right concoction to end it all. So I took a few handfuls of each substance three different ones to start out and I just swallow them whole and drink a bunch of water. And I just laid there waiting waiting to fall asleep waiting for the shortness of breath waiting to suffocate waiting for something to happen besides pain. I laid there didn't even write a suicide note because there was no need for one everyone knew my life was a disaster and I lost everything that mattered to me.. I didn't even write a suicide letter cuz I know everyone knew my life was a disaster and there was nothing left to say. I lost everything that mattered to me. So I said one last pair and said father please let this be it take me now I don't want to be here anymore.

The next day my head was pounding I opened my eyes and completely defeated I was still alive and now awake. You've got to be kidding me why am I still here. I don't want to be here anymore I have nothing left to offer and nobody wants me. And yet somehow I'm stuck on planet Earth it's just an empty f****** soul I just laid there there's nothing to do no reason to get out of bed and I couldn't even succeed at finishing my at ending my life. I've always been a woman of many plans so I counted this is my first attempt. If you want to succeed at anything you have to first forego many field attempts it's one thing I've learned very early in life so the next day still defeated still numb incapable of feeling anything but loss and grief I went to work did my job came home ate some food and try it again. And again I woke up so I don't really disappointed that I was still alive I woke up. I tried this night after night for 2 weeks some nights my heart will be beating so fast I actually couldn't fall asleep so I would keep taking more medication hopefully hoping it would knock me out but all I could feel is my heart beating out of my chest. The more medication I took the less sleep I was getting. I thought it would be the other way around it would knock me out but my heart would just pound so fast and so hard that kept me awake. Once I realized that I was not going to succeed at killing myself and I was making myself more miserable by taking more doses of the cocktail in the beginning and throughout the night just trying to die I finally gave up I wasn't able to kill myself I didn't know how. And even if I did I had a quiet feeling inside of me that God wouldn't let me die. They do say it does happen is in his time and for the first time I actually believe it I've never tried so hard so many times to kill myself and not able to. I remember it was Christmas day I was scheduled to work and my mental health is so bad I need a child I was caring for would not be safe in my hands. I thought I would be okay and that I could handle it but the day Christmas came 3 hours before I was supposed to go into work I knew there was no way I was mentally stable to go in. So I did what any good nurse would do, I called off work to protect the patient. My mental health was so bad I couldn't think straight, I couldn't see straight and the tears kept falling. I was in no shape to care for another person since I couldn't care for myself. Following day my employer called me notified me that the family fired me. I knew that was a consequence that could was a potential consequence but for me I would much rather get fired for protecting my client then keep my job and something bad happened to the client because I wasn't able to perform. So I made the sacrifice called off and lost my job, but I knew I did the right thing because that child was safe because I wasn't there. We all make sacrifices in life and some people never know what they are, but I know for me as long as I can look at myself at the end of the day and know that I did the best I could for all the right reasons that was good enough.

Well I'm going to be stuck living I might as well find a reason to live. Anytime I ask my mom or anyone else what they live for it's always for their kids. Here I am 30 years old and I don't have any kids. But I could become a foster parent. So that's what I did I started classes to become a foster parent at a local agency. I at least had a reason to wake up every day something new to learn possibly someone to help. After all that's what all the recovery programs teach me is to be a maximum usefulness to God into my fellows. So here we go here's something else.

It took about 6 months to a year I got my foster care license. That time frame I felt enough stamina to start working with a new family and home health Care, buy a house, and trade in my Toyota solara convertible car for a white four-door Toyota Prius I know I would need to be a foster parent. I my cousin Jake moving temporarily while he found another place to live. It was going to be another 6 months before placement anyway so why not help out a fellow family member and bring an additional income at the same time. Little did I know my sex addiction was at play.

My cousin Jake successfully moved in a couple weeks later. He's working full-time just got out of a relationship so everything looked simple from the outside.. periodically around the house the door would need fixed a bathroom drain would need tended to and he loved to cook. So the next thing I knew between watching him fix things in his work pants still told boots and wife beater the feelings started. I didn't know I'm really growing up the only thing I knew was he went from house to house. Periodically and Foster Care and I saw him maybe two Christmases out of my whole childhood. And now he's a man a good looking hard-working charismatic man… Also my cousin. I knew it was hands off

Me needing my usual dose of adrenaline every few months decided to go on a trip to the mountains in tennessee. I asked him to go with me. So to Tennessee we went for a 3-day weekend, on our way down we laughed played listen to music told stories and then in the last 2 hours I did one of my favorite moves, I had him take off his shirt while he was driving and I gave him a back massage I always kept oil around for the matter. So here we are 30 minutes and I'm rubbing us back down while we're finishing our 6-hour drive. Before you know it can skin oil down and rubbed all over his back, he misses the exit. We laugh about it and I know it's time to stop cuz we need to get to the cabin. I stopped long enough for him to pull it together and find our way to the cabin. My bag is packed transferred inside we run around hot tub Jacuzzi bath beautiful wood scenery cabin out in the woods it was everything I hoped it would be and more! Then we both sit on the bed throw ourselves back we're both laying on our back staring up free from everything responsibility, family, my last real adventure before I go into parenting full time. He touches my hand and I touched his back accepting his gesture. And he rolls over on top of me and the hot heavy kissing turn into 3 days of bliss.

Oh no what have I done! Well it's too late to take it back now and time to head back to Ohio so after checking out of life and reality for 3 days and pull it together long enough to make the drive back home.

Making are way back to Ohio and submitting to back to our regular responsibilities we had our new relationship as long as we could. I'm slowly it came out cousins found out my mom found out one person at a time people found out that I was committing one of the most disgusting and ear reputable escapades I was participating in incest with my cousin. Realizing I was hooked and could not stop but had to face the world so embarrassed and ashamed but also realizing I have nothing to prove to anybody, we both leave let the world know on Facebook and through standing up for whatever we were doing. I always told myself if I was going to do something do it with pride. Or don't do it at all so I submitted to my addiction full-fledged.

Knowing that he was in a domestic violent felon, not capable of living in the home because of my newfound foster care license, I related party of my bloodline, and the most unstable man I've ever brought into my life. I just couldn't get enough couldn't get enough of the unpredictability, the excitement, the adventure, and the rebellion in me that love pissing off the world by being true to myself. And its own sick way I was living my Bliss by repelling my own family and the church that so aggressively let me down for 18 years of childhood.

Then after careful set of interviews and home studies, I passed all the criteria received my foster license and was placed with my first 15 year old girl,. It was 2 years of undreamable trauma. One child was drugged by her own mom on visitation, it was confirmed with a urine drug screen at the ER after the visit. Then children services decided to continue unsupervised visit with parent. I submitted and gave the child up I was not going to deal with a child that I've been drugged by our own mom and then told it could happen again. I didn't have a stamina to deal with all the trauma of the child and the trauma the parent put on that child and to continue with unsupervised visits. That's like a 4-day nightmare a day before the visitation, the visitation and today 2 to 3 days after to recover from the abuse. My role is a foster parent with literally to pick up the pieces of the parents that left their child on attended I and unloved. I noticed neglect was the main of use over the course of 2 years. Most of the kids were left completely unattended while parents were out on s*********, drug usage or alcohol abuse. All the while I was running a household trying to keep my significant others temper from breaking things around the house and pushing me down in the bedroom or dragging me down the steps outside so he could scream at me at night. Oh and of course there's the accusations of me cheating on him every time somebody looks at me. So now my inner core and shell was dying trying to battle the abuse in temper tantrums of my significant other, and Foster kids. My body started shutting down, I was tired I could barely get out of bed to get the kids ready for school my face swollen from holding all my feelings and not knowing what to do about it, and my only hope was at least I have a reason to wake up today so I won't kill myself. What a way to live. I'm not going to kill myself for the sole reason that I'm going to help somebody else. Even my reason for living was codependent. Every time Jake would have an outburst start breaking things screaming at me and pushing me around the house I would give him minutes to leave or I would call the police. Already being a convicted felon if he goes back to prison it's for a 10-year sentence minimum. So I knew how to get him out of the house unfortunately he couldn't live there so he had no rights. But for some reason the going would get tough, the kids would become too much, I would be overwhelmed with anger confusion and hurt, and I needed something to call me down. I needed sex I had to have sex to survive the hell hole I've created in my life.

CHAPTER 11

ATTACHMENT

After reliving a vicious cycle of abuse first honeymoon second tension building third outburst and 4th relief release in calm after reliving this cycle for 2 years the Foster company notified me at the end of my parenting that they would no longer place kids with me. Begging for a reason to live I asked what their reason was. They notified me and told me I wasn't capable of attaching to the kids and that was their main concern. Attachment was attachment have to do with anything. The kids had a roof over their head food I tried to make myself available if they needed them to talk to and I wanted them to have a social life and participate in school activities. What was I missing I'm so confused what is attachment why would I need to attach I don't understand.

So here I am 35 years old. Severely neglected in childhood, prayed on in my teenage years for sexual encounters, and my twenties I found a way to survive by taking off my clothes for a living to meet my basic needs, then needed a new career after a recession and became a nurse my late twenties I finally settled down and got married only to have my husband leave me after to miscarriages and a dead sister. Trying to find any reason to live and give back to the community my bright idea was to become a foster parent try to care about kids now they're telling me I can't even do that. I can't stop being raped and abused by men , now I have kids abusing me, and now they won't even let that happen. So here I am 35 years old and any attempt to have a relationship I am just epically destroyed trying to just spread my love and compassion. And I can't even do that successfully. I have no reason to live I don't even want to live, but I'm too chickenshit to kill myself and even when I did try to kill myself it didn't work, so now what do I do what do I f****** do with my life. I am so lost.

Somewhere along the grief and depression of being told that I can't even get paid to have to be abused by children services in foster kids. I finally found the chapter ecclesiastics everything in life is meaningless. Every single thing in life is meaningless I have traveled the United States I made more money that I can count, I've had more men then I could imagine, I was in newspapers magazines then I get into a professional sophisticated field where I'm around educated people and well respected and desired, I married an amazing man you have lots of money but he left me because he was using me too. Now I I let the government use me for room and board on top of a domestic violent felon use me for room and board and sex and now they won't even stay with me my whole life is a complete hopeless cause no one will stay with me no one will love me and I have no reason to live. Everything in life is meaningless, so if everything in life is meaningless what's the f****** point and then at the end of the chapter it said enjoy your life. When you've done it all seen it all heard it all you have nothing left to offer but you have everything to offer all at the same time life is just meaningless so f*** it enjoy your life do whatever you want that brings you Joy.

I's when I finally realized when you're not afraid to die and you've got nothing to prove to anybody that's when you really start to live! Just go live your life and enjoy what you're doing and the people you're around.

So that's exactly what I did. I bought a brand new pontoon boat and I started taking it on the water, I went to the beach three times that year which is a lot when you live in Ohio, and I just learned to take care of myself and enjoy my life. I realized something in the process. I have yet to find a scenario where I'm not abused by someone. So I decided that celibacy and being in love with myself and married to myself is my happily ever after. I have a wonderful dog Abby that gives me all the love and affection that I need the 5 A's attention affection allow acceptance appreciation. I am safe when I'm alone and I have all the love I need because God loves me and I love myself. I have the ABCs of attachment acceptance and belonging in my recovery programs, comfort from God my dog and myself, and safety because when I'm alone it is the safest place for me. Peace and happiness is the most important thing in my life. And when I let live my life in solitude and celibacy I have all the peace and happiness I want. Yes it would be amazing to share the wonderful moments with another person and to get the support I need during the tough times because that's what relationships are for to enhance the good times and to support you in the bad times, but I haven't found someone that could do that yet. With the life that I've lived for some reason being comforted and supported as a skill that so many people don't have. So I perfected the ability to enjoy the wonderful times with God and get support that I need in the tough times from god. So I guess I'm not in solitude to marry God I decided I want to be God's bride. God loves me unconditionally the same way I'm able to love so many people, that's what I deserve and that's what I need and he's only one who's capable of giving it to me the way that I need. He gives me everything I could ever ask for and with the right amount of humility I always feel like I have everything I could ever want. I've even made love to God in my own way and he makes love to me. So my happy ending is I fell in love with myself and with God and that is the perfect blessing to live for every day. And my purpose in life is to take care of myself and love and respect other people. And I love to love people because I know what it feels like to be in pain and to be angry and confused and scared and violated and tormented humiliated and hungry. I know it so much pain feels like and when I see someone in pain and I get the chance to love them through that it is the most unbelievable blessing. I never could have imagined all the pain I've got been through could actually benefit my life but it does. Because now when I'm able to love other people through their pain that's when God loves me the most I can feel his love through these people through their wounds through their sadness through their loss. Being able to hold them through that spiritually emotionally and physically is the most beautiful gift I've ever been given. It's like Christmas everyday in my heart when I get to love people and god holds my hand kisses me on the forehead every night and reminds me Lisa everything's going to be okay.

So some people may Wonder how am I going to have sex who am I going to make love to. Well I realize now sex is a physical way of expressing an emotional and spiritual love and commitment. And I realize I can do that with God. I love God so much that I'm going to physically emotionally and spiritually love all of his people everyday. And that is my way of having sex and I get to have sex all day all the time with the world I just have to do it in a way that's not physical. I make love to the world every day all the time and that makes me happy. And peace and happiness is all that matters. God loves me I love me I love God and I love the world so much. I get to have intercourse because I open up my heart and I let God inside of me. And I make love to him by loving his people. So being a sex addict is the greatest thing that ever happened to me because everything I've been through the sexual assaults, sexual abuse, rapes and incest has all given me one thing a greater ability to love other people that have gone through this too. So because of my trauma I can now give back to the world and love the world that much more because I know what it feels like to be in those situations and the feel like I don't matter nobody cares about me and all they want is to use me and I have to have them so I feel important. I know what that feels like cuz I felt that way for 36 years and now I know that someone's supposed to care about me, there's supposed to care about how I feel. Wow what a revolution. So grateful I finally found my groom, God!

> There's one warning I have found and being a loving person. That when you love yourself and God loves you, you are capable of loving everybody. So for me I fall in love all the time everyday with whoever's right in front of me and it's a beautiful thing. Having said that people will fall in love with the feeling they get when they're loved. Because oxytocin is produced. When someone feels wanted and loved oxytocin is produced in the

brain. And when oxytocin is produced in the brain and someone has an experienced that before it becomes an addiction because once you feel loved and wanted for the first time you have to have more of it. So being a loving person you become the addiction. Because when someone eats sugary food oxytocin is produced in the brain, when someone has sex oxytocin is produced in the brain, when someone drinks alcohol oxytocin is produced in the brain, when someone takes narcotics oxytocin is produced in the brain, when someone gambles and wins oxytocin is produced in the brain, when someone feels loved and wanted oxytocin is produced in the brain. So when you become a loving person you become an addiction that everyone will want and not be able to get enough of, and that's why loving people are so abused because the needy people that are desperate for love and feeling wanted become addicted to that person. And people who are not in recovery are not safe and are very abusive. And that's why I've been abused my whole life because I was raised and lived in a world full of addicts that never got help. And because I've been there and I've been one I understand and I can love them through it, but if they're not working a program that I'm going to get abused and continue being abused. There's no way around it addicts are not kind are not safe people. They just hide it really well.